A Little Book of
DUMB QUESTIONS

A Little Book of

DUMB QUESTIONS

MICHAEL POWELL

BOXTREE

First published 2001 by Boxtree
an imprint of Pan Macmillan Ltd
Pan Macmillan, 20 New Wharf Road, London N1 9RR
Basingstoke and Oxford
Associated companies throughout the world
www.panmacmillan.com

ISBN 0 7522 6150 9

10

A CIP catalogue record for this book is available from
the British Library.

Typeset by Dan Newman/Perfect Bound Ltd

Printed by The Bath Press, Bath

Dumb questions have challenged humankind since the inventor of the wheel was first asked 'so when are you going to add the corners?'

It has been said that an infinite number of typing monkeys would eventually create all the great works of literature. While the monkeys haven't written a word of Shakespeare yet, they have managed to produce this little book of startling philosophical insights.

Here are the dumbest and yet most strangely profound questions of all time. Some will make you nod, others will make you laugh and the rest will make you grunt noisily as you bang your head against the wall.

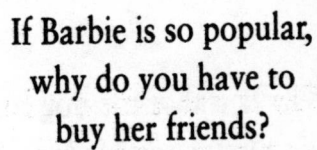

If Barbie is so popular,
why do you have to
buy her friends?

If money is the root of all
evil, why do churches want
it so badly?

Why is it that the dog hates you blowing in his face, but whenever he's in the car he sticks his head out of the window?

Why are wrong numbers
never busy?

Why hasn't someone reported
the Monopolies Commission
to itself?

Why is it called lipstick if you can still move your lips?

How come night falls but day breaks?

Why doesn't Tarzan
have a beard?

Why is the third hand on the watch called a second hand?

Why is lemon juice made with artificial flavour, and washing-up liquid made with real lemons?

Do pilots take crash-courses?

Can you imagine a world with no hypothetical situations?

If cats and dogs didn't have fur, would we still stroke them?

If space is a vacuum, who changes the bags?

If time heals all wounds, how come we have belly buttons?

If swimming is such good exercise, why are whales so fat?

Why do signs that say
'Slow Children' have a picture
of a running child?

How does the snowplough driver get to work in the morning?

If a cow laughed, would milk come out of her nose?

If nothing sticks to Teflon, how do they make Teflon stick to the pan?

If you tied buttered toast
to the back of a cat and
dropped it from a height,
what would happen?

Why can't they make the
planes out of the same
material as the black box?

Why are they called apartments if they're all stuck together?

If the police arrest a mime, do they tell him he has the right to remain silent?

If someone with multiple personalities threatens to kill himself, is it considered a hostage situation?

Why don't sheep shrink
when it rains?

If you ate pasta and
anti-pasta, would they
cancel each other out?

If you try to fail, and succeed,
which have you done?

Do people who are born again
have two belly buttons?

Before they invented
drawing boards, what did
they go back to?

If all the world's a stage,
where is the audience sitting?

What was the best thing
before sliced bread?

If God dropped acid, would
he see people?

If the earth didn't suck, would
we all fall off?

If one synchronized swimmer drowns, do the rest have to drown too?

If you throw a cat out of
the car window, does it
become kitty litter?

If olive oil comes from squeezing olives, how do they make baby oil?

If genetic scientists crossed a chicken with a zebra, would they get a four-legged chicken with its own bar code?

When an agnostic dies, does he go to the 'great perhaps'?

Why is the time of day with the slowest traffic called rush hour?

How do you tell when your bagpipes need tuning?

How come you never hear about gruntled employees?

If practice makes perfect, and nobody's perfect, why practise?

If quitters never win, and winners never quit, should you still quit while you're ahead?

Why is a carrot more orange than an orange?

Why do we wait until a pig is dead to cure it?

After eating, do amphibians have to wait one hour before getting out of the water?

How can there be self-help groups?

If you have a mid-life crisis
while playing hide and seek,
do you automatically lose
because you can't find
yourself?

If you nagged your plants
instead of talking to them,
would they grow, but be
fretful and insecure?

Is there another word for synonym?

What's the word for when you can't remember the word?

Isn't it worrying that doctors call what they do 'practice'?

When sign-makers
go on strike, do they carry
blank picket signs?

When your budgerigar
sees you reading the
newspaper, does he wonder
why you're staring at a
carpet?

Do infants enjoy infancy as much as adults enjoy adultery?

Where do forest rangers go to get away from it all?

If love is blind, why is lingerie so popular?

Why are haemorrhoids called
'haemorrhoids' instead of
'asteroids'?

Why is the alphabet
in that order? Is it because of
that song?

Does killing time damage
eternity?

If God sneezed,
what would you say?

Whose cruel idea was it for the word 'lisp' to have an 's' in it?

Can you be a closet
claustrophobic?

If a man talks in a forest and
there is no woman there to
contradict him, is he still
wrong?

If a stealth bomber crashed in a forest, would it make a sound?

If people from Poland are called Poles, why aren't people from Holland called Holes?

Why do we say something is out of whack? What's a whack?

If aliens are intelligent enough to travel billions of miles through space, why do they keep abducting the dumbest people on Earth?

How much deeper would the sea be without sponges?

If ignorance is bliss, why aren't more people happy?

Are part-time bandleaders
semiconductors?

When companies
ship Styrofoam, what do they
pack it in?

Could someone ever get
addicted to counselling?
How could you treat them?

Daylight saving time – why are they saving it and where do they keep it?

Doesn't 'expecting the unexpected' make the unexpected expected?

Five years from now, will they have a Soviet Reunion?

How did a fool and his money
get together in the first place?

How do 'Keep Off the Grass' signs get where they are?

How do you know honesty is the best policy, if you haven't tried all the other options?

How much can we get away
with and still go to heaven?

If a tree falls in a forest and
no one's there to hear it, do
the other trees laugh?

If a tortoise loses its shell,
is it naked or homeless?

If a word in the dictionary
was spelled wrong,
how would we know?

How do you tell
when you've run out of
invisible ink?

Do Procrastinators Anonymous ever arrange a meeting?

If we aren't supposed to
eat animals, why are they
made of meat?

In a country of free speech,
why are there phone bills?

What do little birdies see
when they get knocked
unconscious?

Why do they call it a TV set
when you only get one?

When two aeroplanes almost collide why do they call it a near miss instead of a near hit?

Why do we wash bath towels?
Aren't we clean when we
use them?

Why do we nail down
the lid of a coffin?

Why isn't phonetic spelled the
way it sounds?

Do you realize how many
holes there could be if people
bothered to take the dirt out
of them?

Why isn't there more than one
in every crowd?

Do hummingbirds hum
because they've forgotten the
words?

How do you 'draw a blank'?

Is drilling for oil boring?

If rabbits' feet are so lucky, then what happened to the rabbit?

Is there something you can take for kleptomania?

Why are violets blue and not violet?

If you're in Hell and you're angry with someone, where do you tell them to go?

Why do croutons come in airtight packages? It's already stale bread.

When cheese gets its picture taken, what does it say?

What's the speed of dark?

Are people more violently opposed to fur rather than leather because it's much easier to harass rich women than motorcycle gangs?

Should a crematorium give discounts for burn victims?

Why do they sterilize the needles for lethal injections?

What if the lid of a milk carton said 'Open somewhere else'?

If 75 per cent of all accidents happen within five miles of home, why don't we all move ten miles away?

Why is it called a bust, when
it stops right before the part it
is named after?

Is it possible to be totally
partial?

Why is the word abbreviation
so long?

When you choke a Smurf, what colour does he turn?

Have you considered that
with enough people, ropes,
duct tape and electricity,
you actually could lead
a horse to water and make
it drink?

Do radioactive cats have
eighteen half lives?

Why do they put expiration dates on sour cream containers?

If Hare Krishnas start cloning themselves how will the rest of us find out?

Why is it so hard to remember
how to spell 'mnemonic'?

If vampires can't see their own reflections, why is their hair always so tidy?

Why do tugboats push?

Do bleached blondes pretend
to have more fun?

Why don't they call
moustaches 'mouthbrows'?

Did God invent alcohol
so ugly people can have
sex too?

If you jog backwards,
do you gain weight?

Are Cheerios really
doughnut seeds?

Do stars clean themselves with
meteor showers?

If I have sex with my clone,
will I go blind?

If the pen is mightier than the sword, and a picture is worth a thousand words, how dangerous is a fax?

Why do people steal hotel towels when hundreds of people have used them to dry their crotches?

Why do people without a
watch look at their wrist
when you ask them what time
it is?

If everything is part of
a whole, what is the whole
part of?

If man evolved from apes,
what are apes for?

In court, why do they ask if you swear to tell the truth? If you're planning on lying, do they really think you'll tell them?

Can sexual harassment at work be a problem if you're self-employed?

What if Hell really did freeze over? What would we use instead?

What if the hokey cokey really
is what it's all about?

If gifts are free,
what is a 'free' gift?

What makes cheese so
confidential that we actually
need cheese shredders?

When dog food is new and improved tasting, how do they know?

When they first invented the clock, how did they know what time to set it to?

Where does your lap go when you stand up?

Why aren't there ever any guilty bystanders?

If beauty is only skin deep, do ugly people look attractive if you remove their skin?

If all generalizations are false,
is this one true?

Is today a day for making firm decisions?

Is it bad luck to believe in superstition?

For someone with a memory like a sieve, is thinking a straining process?

Are Santa's little helpers
subordinate clauses?

If today is the first day of the rest of your life, what was yesterday?

Aren't rooms always at room temperature?

Do cannibals leave the table
after everyone's eaten?

If God were a woman, would
sperm taste like chocolate?

If the universe is expanding,
why can't you ever find a
parking space?

Is a Zebra twenty-six times
larger than an 'A' bra?

At what point in a relationship is it OK to stop wiping your arse?

Is reading on the toilet multi-tasking?

If the meek are going to inherit the earth, why don't they look more smug about it?

Who needs a silk purse
when you've got this really
cool pig's ear?

Michael Powell grew up in North Wales where his hobbies included crushing empty beer cans with an anvil and dreaming of what it would be like when he was rich and famous. After gaining an English degree at Manchester University, he trained at RADA and then spent five years as an internationally unknown actor and musical director, before finally packing it all in to become a writer. At an early age he developed an interest in asking dumb questions which is still going strong.
He lives in Somerset with his wife and two young children.